Everyday Magic

poems by

Stacy Russo

Finishing Line Press
Georgetown, Kentucky

Everyday Magic

Copyright © 2019 by Stacy Russo
ISBN 978-1-63534-932-0 First Edition
All rights reserved under International and Pan-American Copyright Conventions. No part of this book may be reproduced in any manner whatsoever without written permission from the publisher, except in the case of brief quotations embodied in critical articles and reviews.

Publisher: Leah Maines

Editor: Christen Kincaid

Cover Art: Stacy Russo

Author Photo: Stacy Russo

Cover Design: Leah Huete

Printed in the USA on acid-free paper.
Order online: www.finishinglinepress.com
also available on amazon.com

Author inquiries and mail orders:
Finishing Line Press
P. O. Box 1626
Georgetown, Kentucky 40324
U. S. A.

Table of Contents

In Another World, I Played 1

I Lived So Hungry for Freedom 2

My Home Became a Woman 3

Just Like You 4

Goddess Spaceship Poem 6

The Glorious Lovers of Shattuck Avenue 8

They are Predicting Light Rain in Vienna 11

The Encyclopedia of Goddesses & Heroines 14

Kate/The Dreamer/South Dakota 17

The Pilgrim 20

Sometimes I'll Listen the Whole Way Through 23

A Full Woman 26

We Were Wild Then/We Carried No Weight 29

In Support of the Violence against Women Act 31

For my brother, David

In Another World, I Played

In another world, I played.
I celebrated my good fortune,
walked as if floating
toward the horizon,
balanced my body
in a blue boat
on the bluest sea
beneath a broad, blue heaven
and evening blue full moons.

In another world, I played.
On a day like any other,
I said a life-changing word: no,
packed my travelling bag,
opened the door,
and crossed over
to live there:
the land of my resurrection.

I Lived So Hungry for Freedom

I lived so hungry for freedom
that you may be surprised by how
I imagined it:
alone, outside, in a field,
eating a large, red,
crisp apple.

During some daydreams,
my eyes closed on my lunch break,
I felt the apple in my hand.
My grip so calm, confident.

The dreams of the non-harmed and safe
may be extravagant, complex.
The dreams of the terrified
are simple.

My Home Became a Woman

My home became a person
while I was away.
Somehow, quite magically,
a woman.
Yes, my home became a woman
with a soft, warm body
in a yellow dress.
A body made of earth
with wide hips
and well-lived feet.

When I returned
to her long, tangled hair
and large, worn artist's hands,
I made coffee,
scrubbed the floors,
polished the countertops,
swept the porch,
and prepared a meal
that I ate outside
from my grandmother's bowl
beneath the moonlight.

Just Like You

I ran my finger
along the index
of a feminist text
and found myself
listed there:
a woman
who dares
to live
alone.

You can find me
on a purple tree-lined street.
My home, near
the curve
with a golden step
leading to
a blue door.

Along with witches, prostitutes,
spinsters, the childless,
tarts, and various
wild women,
I am grouped
with all things
feminine and scary.

The woman
who dares
to live
alone
sets her table-
often a happy, satisfied table
sometimes a lonely, sad table
often a table with no longing
sometimes a table that longs for
      the missing, absent, gone
often a table of laughter and celebration
sometimes a table of a broken heart.

There is nothing curious here.
I set my table
just like you.

Goddess Spaceship Poem

What were you doing
when the goddess spaceship arrived?

I was pulling laundry
from the dryer.
Aunt Carol was
taking out the trash.
Peggy said she was
having a cocktail
to settle her nerves.

Once inside
we saw the messy kitchen,
but no one minded.

Stella, a secretary from Reseda,
was at a magnificent switchboard,
taking calls from reporters
on Earth.

Near the back of the ship,
a glow came
from a compartment
behind a white door.
There we found mom
in a lab coat.

After stretching her arm
in a large, silent arc,
as if opening a ceremony,
she told us,
"I'm being the chemist
I always wanted."

My hips were rounder.
Peggy had a soft belly.
Aunt Carol's scar
above her right eye,
no longer hidden behind foundation,
was luminous and diamond-shaped.
I knew we were in our
true bodies.

When dinner came,
we gathered outside,
women stretched in waves
as a rainbow ocean
north south
east west.

Mom took a break
from the lab
to join us.
She sat next to me
on a silver chair,
drinking champagne
from a ruby chalice.
Her gray hair
glowed radiantly
with an azure sky
behind her.

She leaned over
and whispered to me,
"I knew this would happen, baby.
Here we are together
living the dream."

The Glorious Lovers of Shattuck Avenue

Last month, Anna,
the anarchist librarian,
retired from her post
at age 68.
"I will have more time
to devote to my romance,"
she told us.

A round woman
with hair like a bush of wires,
Anna often wears
something that resembles
an art school smock
with large square pockets
in the front.
She keeps a revolutionary
pamphlet or two
stashed inside.

She is
our local
Emma Goldman.

Leonard, a radical
within walking distance
of the branch,
visited often.
Twenty years younger
than Anna,
it surprised us
when they
moved in together.

"How does it feel
to find love
at your age?"
I asked her.
She replied
with her hands
resting in her
front pockets—
her stare with me
and beyond:
"Glorious."

Last Sunday I was walking
down Shattuck
when I saw Anna and Leonard
in the old Laundromat.
You may not believe me
when I tell you,
but they were dancing.
He twirled and dipped her.
I felt like a voyeur,
but couldn't stop watching
their urban spectacle
of romance.

Maybe I've
never seen
a man
so devoted.

Anna placed her hands
flat on Leonard's chest,
arched her head back.
Her large breasts
rolled like domes
atop the pockets
of her smock.

The fluorescent lights
gave her bush-like hair
a golden, perfect, illuminated,
heavenly halo.

The spinning clothes.
The other spectators.
The freedom of it all.
The revelation of possibilities
in the bend of Leonard's arms.
Sunday evening.
9:40 p.m., 61 degrees.
Berkeley, California.
The glorious lovers
of Shattuck Avenue.

They Are Predicting Light Rain in Vienna

My grandfather, Pete,
a used car salesman
from Bellflower,
only got the paper
for the weather page.
There on his lot
of clunkers and
an occasional, rare beauty,
he'd sit in his dusty shack
each morning,
smoking Pall Malls
and studying
the weather.

Surf predictions
from Point Conception
to Mexico.
LA Basin temperatures
and those of
certain California cities:
San Francisco, Monterey, Laguna Beach.
Until he reached
his favorite part:
the world.
Walking the lot,
high on whiskey, tobacco, and caffeine,
he gave useless information
to his customers.

"Can you believe
it was 102 in Havana yesterday?"

"Rome has held steady
at 81 degrees for three days."

"They are predicting
light rain in Vienna."

At age 78 he packed
his junked Cadillac
and drove with his
third wife
to Stanley, Idaho,
for a weeklong vacation.
In the driveway,
a few minutes before his departure,
my dad said,
"I've never heard of it."
Pete, the explorer, took a long drag
off his Pall Mall.
Behind a cloud of smoke,
he informed us,
"According to the *LA Times*,
Stanley is the coldest place
in the states most days."

There are other things
I could tell you
about my family.
Like how my mom,
a marginal cook,
pasted recipes from magazines
on sky blue construction paper
from an art store
in Orange County
or how my dad
had a subscription
to *Organic Gardening,*
but we never had a garden.

On a bad day
when I feel I have little
to stand on,
I stop myself.
Consider all who are gone
and what they left me.
I imagine
the old Cadillac
making its journey
to Stanley,
my dad closely
examining *Organic Gardening*
at the kitchen table,
and my mom
on the midnight couch
surrounded by Elmer's glue,
scissors, and sky blue paper.

It's enough
for me
to tell others
I come from
a family of dreamers.

The Encyclopedia of Goddesses & Heroines

When a lull settles
over the reference desk,
the librarians order books,
grade papers, or
organize thick stacks of work
they carry
from their offices,
but Jane reads entries
from the *Encyclopedia of
Goddesses & Heroines.*

Like all great books,
it has no ending
or beginning.

She reads of Venus
ruling over herbs
and cypress trees
and the summer goddess
worshipped by
the people
of San Juan, New Mexico.

On occasion
she now misses her stop
on the bus ride home.
There amongst the clamor
of activity,
long faces,
bitter realities,
shuffling feet,
bags,
empty coffee containers,
uniforms,
failures,
hopes,

new loves,
and
broken hearts,
Jane quietly sits
and ponders
her heroines:
bear women,
water goddesses,
a tall Cherokee
who wishes to marry
a hummingbird,
and her secret favorite:
a woman
the sun
so loved
that he dropped
a golden swing
to pull her up
to his home.

She imagines a
Native American earth mother
who made love
with the sky
and gave birth
to the mountains.
She read of the earth mother's
four wombs.
She dreams of what
may be planted there
in the four wombs.
What may take hold
and bloom.
Be it wild or tame.
Red or violet.

And how it would feel
to be inside
and enter the world
from those four
divine chambers.

Jane has
never revealed
to even
her closest confidants
that she believes
it may all
be true.

And if given
the chance
to sit
on the golden swing
she would go
with the sun.

In bed
alone
late at night
with her alarm clock set
she can
almost feel
the heat on her arms
and the warmth
against her face
as she rises
and the sun pulls.

Kate/The Dreamer/South Dakota

Kate, age 48,
outside Rapid City,
can usually sense
when her neighbor
is in the alley.
She watches
from her bedroom window
on tiptoes
to take him in, full.
Sitting on the tailgate
of his Dodge,
smoking cigarettes
with the moon.
His long legs
dangling far
in tan work boots.
"He must be six-two,"
she once whispered
to herself.

Sometimes she hears
him on the phone.
"I'm an outdoor enthusiast,"
he said,
and, "Come on, Donna!"
another time.
She hears his closet door
sliding on the track,
the opening and closing
of his front door,
late night TV,
running water,
and little else.

Kate became a dreamer
when she was young,

but now,
middle-aged,
her dreams are broad, thick-
deep enough
to soak up
her boring days
at the market.

She hangs ornaments,
glass globes and stars-
red, green, blue-
on the trees
around her
small place and
asks customers
in the check-out line
puzzling questions:

"What do you think
it's like
in Paris
right now?"

"How many tents,
do you suppose,
are on Mt. Everest
today?"

When her boyfriend
comes over-
she places
heart-shaped cookies
on a metallic platter,
paints her toenails
fire engine red,

makes sure her
bra and panties match
and her socks are
without holes,
but when he talks
about his day,
what movies are playing
in town,
she drifts,
her ears tilted
toward the shared wall
for hints
of the man
next door.
She doesn't want to miss
the muffled sounds,
long legs,
occasional phone calls,
running water
in the kitchen sink
or shower
of the mysterious
outdoor enthusiast.

The Pilgrim

In her middle years,
Rita, a rare book cataloger,
developed a thing for Henry Miller.
She is the only librarian
in the whole county,
perhaps the state,
who can quote
long passages
from *Crazy Cock*.

Last May,
four years widowed,
she visited
where Henry
used to live
in Big Sur.

She drove her green van
up Highway 1.
Scattered books,
chocolate donuts,
peanut butter,
whole wheat bread,
and two quarts of water
rolled around
in the back.

In what she considered
the spirit of Henry
she wore a flowered skirt
with no underwear.

It was her 50th year.

Outside LA, she thought,
"I'm on a pilgrimage."
Passing Santa Barbara,
it shortened to,
"I'm on pilgrimage."
Near Ragged Point,
a gas station attendant,
asked about
her destination.
She stepped from the van,
turned her body
in a full circle
and simply told him,
"pilgrimage."

When Rita reached
the Henry Miller Library,
she sat on the front deck
with other travelers.
She ate peanut butter
from a jar
with a plastic spoon,
gazed at the redwoods,
the blue sky,
the dirty soles
of her feet.
A few rows of white chairs
stretched across the lawn.
"There was a wedding last night,"
a man's voice said.
The peanut butter
filled her mouth
in a satisfying way,
so she closed
her eyes.

Rita camped close by that night.
In her tent
she dreamed
of white chairs,
the lawn,
the coastline.
She saw the faces
of the travelers.
Her feet moved
against the soft interior
of her sleeping bag.

Like any good pilgrim,
her soul had an even beat.

In the morning,
she ate chocolate donuts
on the front deck
of the library,
gathered her skirt
in her lap,
and pondered
the meaning
of her journey.

Sometimes I'll Listen the Whole Way Through

While I was waiting
by the pay phone
for Tom that last time,
I counted the change
in my pocket.
Then I started counting
the lines on my left palm.

"Kathleen," he yelled
through the open window
when he pulled up,
"This has to stop!"
I saw he was wearing
his work uniform.

This was
long before
I got clean.
Years before
I learned to surf,
travelled to Mexico,
saw beyond myself,
found peace.
At least
a decade
before I could
love a man,
completely.

I was unhinged with him.
Loose.
A black-out drunk.

In his truck that day
The Pretenders' "My City Was Gone"
played low.
His eyes
had shadows
when he looked
at me.

Whenever I hear
that song,
all these years later,
I see
his young, tired eyes.
The uniform.
His left hand
clutching the wheel.
I feel the finality
of it all.

Sometimes I'll listen
the whole way through,
let the emotions
seep in.
It's not
an easy thing
to do.

I have no idea
where he lives,
or how his life
turned out, but
I've thought of
finding him.

To thank him
for cleaning my wounds,
brushing off the dirt,
putting me
back together.

Rubbing the soles
of my feet.

Combing my hair.

The kindness
he gave me.

All he offered.

The strong,
silent beauty,
I've come
to realize,
that he
possessed.

A Full Woman

The first few months
of the separation,
living in my new place,
I'd get restless
in the evenings.
It was worse,
being winter.
I couldn't walk
around the neighborhood
in the dark,
so I'd drive
to the thrift store
a mile down the road.

There were other people
inside like me–
regulars, alone
with nowhere to go.
I whispered a few times
to the cashiers,
"I'm going through
a divorce."

I bought glass, ceramic
orbs, vases, bottles
in shades of blue, green,
some clear, a few
tinted red
and then I moved
onto bowls,
about a dozen–
all wood, smooth
different sizes.

I kept the objects on the floor
near my bed
in boxes I scavenged
from behind the store.
I'd sort them
when I got home.
Polish them.
It kept me busy.
It felt important.

At night,
by the moonlight,
I'd see them glow-
lighting the floor.

One day I called
my brother over.
He was good
at building things.
He worked on my patio
most of the day.
We shared a six-pack.
Listened to 70s music.

We moved the shelves
he constructed
into the living room-
alongside a tall wall
that the sun hit
every afternoon.
I arranged the objects there.

I went to the store
a few more times.
Then I lost the need.

I'd sit,
admiring the collection
spread out on the shelves.
They were things of beauty, comfort,
holding a silent energy.
Perhaps a message.

By the time
summer came around,
I was a new woman.
No longer pacing.
I was balanced, open-
no longer afraid
of the night.

I discovered
I have something
in me-
I feel it burning
in there.
I can chart things out.
Determine my destiny.
Plan, proceed.
I've realized who and what
I am.
My possibilities.
A full woman.

We Were Wild Then/We Carried No Weight

All those years ago
at Annie's Culver City home-
that marvelous place
with its tiny red bathroom,
purple curtains,
and a porch of
sun yellow tiles-
you could stretch
out your legs
and voice your secrets and wishes
with a confident ease
in the back lot
between two avocado trees
that bent sideways
toward each other
and an old lemon tree
we called Fran.

The gang we were
rode our bikes barefoot
to the corner market.
Riding back through
the warm night alleys,
I yelled,
"What will become of us?"
and Annie would point
toward the stars-
her arms wide open.
Her generous
exposed heart.

We were wild then.
We carried no weight.

Once in that
avocado-laden lawn
beneath Fran's fertile canopy
Annie brought out
her deck
to give us each
a reading.
In her hands,
turned toward me
in ceremony,
my future card:
the nine of cups.
I felt my chest and belly swell
in anticipation
of the good
and the fullness
the card promised.

In my later years,
even though
I've been more hungry
than full and caught a hollowness
along the way that
I can't shake,
this memory remains
as an old friend.
Some nights
I sleep deep within it,
because in that moment
I felt a rare thing.
I believed completely
in each bend
of my young body
that I was blessed,
that I had gifts,
that a fortune awaited me.

In Support of the Violence against Women Act

Around age 40, she stopped being a savior of men.
First she travelled to the forest.
Then she went to the desert.
Later she sat in her car and looked out at the ocean.
Finally, she stayed home.
She planted trees, sunflowers, lavender, sage.
She bought heavy plates and cups.
She stocked her pantry
with more tea than she could ever drink.
She kept an entire shelf for chocolate.
She sat at her own table.
She ate whatever she wanted.
She kept her hair unkempt.
And when the days ended,
she left things unclean
and she slept.
She welcomed sleep like a kind, distant lover.
She slept without fear of being awakened.
She slept without fear of the next day.
She slept without fear of doing the wrong thing.
She slept a sleep she had longed for.
She slept eight, ten, twelve hours.
She slept upstairs.
She slept downstairs.
She slept wherever she pleased.
She slept under thick blankets from Mexico.
She slept under a cool, soft, white sheet.
She slept with the blinds closed tied.
She slept with the blinds wide open.
She slept in the morning, evening, and afternoon.
She slept with sounds of the California freeway.
Sounds of singing birds.
Sounds of heavy December rain against the roof and windows.
Sounds of neighbors returning late from parties.
Sounds of her passed mother's voice.
Sounds of her passed father brewing his 5 a.m. coffee.

Sounds of places visited and places to go.
Sounds of her solitude.
She slept in the dark.
She slept in the sunlight.
She slept in poetry.
She slept the most peaceful sleep imaginable.

Stacy Russo, a librarian and professor at Santa Ana College in Santa Ana, California, is a writer, poet, and artist. She believes in libraries as community spaces; lifelong learning; peaceful living; and the power of personal story. Her book publications include *Love Activism* (Litwin Books); *We Were Going to Change the World: Interviews with Women from the 1970s/1980s Southern California Punk Rock Scene* (Santa Monica Press); *Life as Activism: June Jordan's Writings from The Progressive* (Litwin Books); and *The Library as Place in California* (McFarland). She is currently working on a collection of interviews titled *A Better World Starts Here: Activists and Their Work* (forthcoming, Sanctuary Publishers). Her articles, poetry, and reviews have appeared in *Feminist Teacher, Feminist Collections, American Libraries, Counterpoise, Library Journal, Chaffey Review, Serials Review,* and the anthology *Open Doors: An Invitation to Poetry* (Chaparral Canyon Press). *Everyday Magic* is her first poetry collection. *The Moon and Other Poems* is forthcoming from Dancing Girl Press.

Stacy was born in Harrisburg, Pennsylvania, and lived outside the city until her family moved to Southern California in 1981. She grew up as a teenager in the punk rock scene of the 1980s, which she credits for her political awakening and do-it-yourself ethic. She believes everyone has the power to create. Stacy holds degrees from the University of California, Berkeley; Chapman University; and San Jose State University. Contact Stacy and discover more about her work at www.love-activism.com.

www.ingramcontent.com/pod-product-compliance
Lightning Source LLC
LaVergne TN
LVHW041600070426
835507LV00011B/1218